Prophecy in
BRIDGEPORT
and other poems

Prophecy in BRIDGEPORT
and other poems
BY AL LEVINE
CHARLES SCRIBNER'S SONS NEW YORK

11/1972
Genl.

To Julie and Jonny and Water's Edge Road

CONTENTS

Even your lessons
Basho
Are only foot-prints

AND IF I HAVE RELEASED THE DEAD

For Jack Unterecker

The poem I was going to send you
Changed in my hand as I set it
The smooth stone becoming rough
The laterite changing to a yellow olivine
The tale about the witch in the woods
To a princess weaving about her tower
A baffle of bronze threads
The wolf-gate to a yellow-grayish mist
The sores of the dead man
Reforged by Khalkeos the Smith
The living walking above the dead
As on a roof
The dead princess in hell
Pulling down the roots of the asphodel
The bronze fortune
Freezing to a ringing gold
The golden barrow melting
Like the dead snow

And if I have released the dead,
Fortune
Follows

You asked me whether or not
The myths remained
Alive somewhere
And we answered you
Tonight
More deeply asleep
Than even your dreams follow
You beheld
Us
Who will carry you strongly

1

To the end of the sky
When your grave is blown
From beneath its soft encloset
Covering

YOUR STORY

You told me how Caligula had looked for you
And Macro, the colonel in chief of the Praetorian Guard
Had put a reward on your head of ten thousand sesterces
And how you had lost yourself in the Armenian quarter
           on the top floor of an insula
Being afraid to come out except at night
And how the Emperor had expressed a desire to see your head
With two Celtic nose-flutes in the nostrils
And a pneumatic machine pumping air through the neck-hole
And how the Emperor had pissed on Macro's foot when he
           couldn't find you.
And how Macro had smiled and planted the dagger in his soul
Which grew into the German war sword that split
           Caligula's abdomen like a lobster
And how by this time you had left Rome for Dalmatia
And how you went swimming near Split when the
           Ninth Legion was on your trail
And how the fish covered up the hole that you made in
           the Adriatic when you dove to the bottom
And how Pythagoras the Philosopher was waiting for you there
And how the tones of a lute in sea water are three octaves
           lower than they are on land
And how old you are now
And how your apartment here in Naples costs
           you practically nothing

Somehow I believe you.

2

GREEKS IN PERSIA

This language, which once was the language of kitchen gardens,
Of small white houses shining in the sun like the baby teeth
             of the mountains,
Now is lost in the gray winds of this great plain,
Swirled between the hooves of the king's horses
As the wind carries it away.
The word: bread, the word: sister, the word: sleep
Carried through this unsleeping void,
These are sounds as small as the stars in the night
Or the pebbles that roll with the storm
Or the sands that fling themselves against our cheeks.
How closely a few olive trees could fill the tiny valleys
             when the spring leaves sang.

3

One of the rowers at Cynossema got a splinter in his hand
And when they put the trophy on the headland, so full to
         the night breeze
That wound which had been merely red had changed to purple
         with a streak of green
Which he could not see until the next morning light,
         although he felt the pain
And though he had been so strong at the oar, the inner man who
         pulls the heavy scull,
The daylight somehow drew in at his mouth, making him
         dream of olives
As the dark color spread along an abcess in his arm
Until by midday he could not pull the joint, was invalided
         on the beach
Along with all the wounded who had punctures, broken ribs,
         and eyes knocked out
And by the following night, after the sunset, when the
         headland rose in the wind,
He dreamt it was bearing him to the dark groves beneath
         the moon of home,
Those silver leaves, tossing in his sleep.

IN A CHURCH IN CHRISTIANSAND, NORWAY

In a church in Christiansand, Norway,
Even Satanas lost faith in man
And he walked among the fishing boats as you would
          on this March ice
And capsized against the black flanks of the mountains:
Those troll steeds:
And they crushed him between their square hooves,

And Egil Skallagrimson, the Hero
Who wanted to slay King Harald
And gave not a shit for the whole court,
He drowned in a meadow and was buried beneath thin turf
And that meager sea was swept bare in the first gales
          of winter,
Coming from the white north

A crazy old man clutching a box of gold
Given by the King of England for service against the Scots
On that day when seven kings fled along the edge of the woods
And he waved his sword through their necks
          as if they were ghosts,
He died of an embolism, blind and without a friend

Both heroes and devils are dead,
Although the heroes weren't much by the time the
          state got through with them.
Not even they or hell itself stood much chance against money,
Which killed them or drove them mad

They say his skull was thick enough to stop the blow of an ax.
They say Egil Skallagrimson was too strong even for
          the saint king,
And they say he killed the cunning men by force and fraud,
But in his weakness he died alone
And the church and the treasury have founded order
          of sunlight on an open grave.

The great hero Egil Skallagrimson refused to
be called a hero
And when he refused he meant it
For he had an ax the size of a whale's fin and the
back to use it with
And a swarthy face like a black fog covering the moon
with an onshore wind
As thick as smoke
The cold fire of the autumn fogs
And his skull, great, bald and riven with the bouncing
strokes of swords and axes
Seemed to swell and fall with the rise of his moods
So that one moment it was a full wandering widow's moon
Glowering over a field of swart blood
And at the next a small cheerful winter sun against the
dark shelf of his shoulders
And his mustache trailed with ragged edges like seaweed
or drifting corpses at the edge of a beach
For dead men are limp.
He was a killer, and yet he was always paying back,
not killing for gain
For some intrigue's ending that would fill his stable with God,
That most ridable steed.
And when the king sent to find him he went overseas,
after killing the men
And he settled near Mosby, north of the bay
And lived for the rest of his life on farm cheese and mutton,
Playing the good but gloomy farmer, and no one
troubled him there.
But when he died it was while carrying the chest of gold
given him by Athelstan
For the death of seven Scottish kings after Thorgrim's death.

Burying it he died, feeble and blind, but with strength
                left in his hands
Caving in the wooden chest as he hugged it, hearing
And feeling the brush of cold steady rain.
It wasn't love of scapula or brooch that made gold his
                death-bride
But a longing for the edge of the wood where he rushed
                forward bravely
Saving his brother's life by craft and courage.
The kiss of treasure is cold, and he'd set himself apart
                by savagery.
But no one praised Skallagrim's son
And his skull, great bald and riven, was as thick as
                ship's hull when they found it buried.
What voyages taken, west and east, were in that head
                before death emptied it,
After a year in the ground.

THERE WERE CERTAIN KIDS . . .

There were certain kids who wanted to be astronomers
Almost before they started
And they climbed to the tops of stone towers
And cast shadows by starlight

The most beautiful thing of all
Is to be an astronomer
More beautiful than the land-fall sea
Or the mid-sea ocean
Or the wave sea on a sloping beach

Sailing stars outside the stars
Like Usodamare and Cadamosto
Who rounded the Cape in the fifteen years before Columbus
In starlight.

More beautiful than King James's fleet
That found the Monopod in California.

More beautiful than Dampier, Von Humboldt and Cook.

More beautiful than the land-fall sea
Is to be an astronomer
In the dawn before dawn
And then to see the energies of God or God-befallen light
Expand like words along the black ecliptic.

There were certain kids who wanted to know the numbers
            of energies
And to press cold stone against their faces,
Endless endless faces of which this universe is the words.
Cold stone cut,
Inscriptions of endless life in death.
Stars like words the most invisible part,
Inscriptions of spaces and night.

THE GRID

It's a well-known fact that the telephone
breeds numbers
And when I called you last night
The numbers had multiplied like rats.

When you were home,
They multiplied so quickly that
I couldn't reach you.

When you weren't home,
One number rang
As long as midnight.

And then,
What symbol is your name?
On what grid were you born?

I know you
Behind your name.
Unreachable.

THE FAIRY TALES

It's dark and cold —
The old brown crow flies through the fields
Pecking at the black cows
And the yellow grass weeps around their hocks
As they run —
A post-Hallowe'en catastrophe.
Color is gone,
The pumpkins have gathered in the barn
To keep warm,
And the farmer spreads his fine manure in the stalls
Hoping to grow pineapples.
I have to laugh
Trudging down the old brown road
With the dogs behind me,
For I see ahead of me
A gigantic birdcage filled with city pimps,
Shivering in their naked plumage.
I wonder,
How many winters are piled up behind the Singer
          sewing machine
In the black shed?
A cow stands across my path and stares,
Asking for small change, while
I stand and finger through my hair
Trying to find money.
She looks creased.

Suddenly the sun breaks out through a rift in the clouds,
Singing like a bird with a yellow throat and a gray breast,
I can hear it as it lights up the unearthly black
          of the shadows
And the cows stop running and listen
While the grass wipes its eyes and sniffles a little and stops
And the crow hangs in mid-air, ashamed of himself,
Leaning on a warm breeze with one wing in amazement,

As the pumpkins knock their heads together in the barn
And the pimps squeeze through the bars and escape naked
Toward the piles of fine duds in the silo.
Screeching ragtag and bobtail songs of delight
To the daliant woods
Which were just about to leave for Vermont but stop and listen
With waving heads
And the new leaves stretching with delight from their twigs
As they dance,
And everyone is together for a while
While the sun shines
And winter stops bitching its eternally depressive wind.
The cow says forget it
And runs toward the bull.
I find a ten spot in my hat
and light my cigar with it.
The dogs eat the pork chops
That fall out of my ass
And lick my hand for it.
The sun dries my hand for it.
It's warm and bright.

DANCING TOGETHER

Is this some sort of sacred round?
Round dances went out with the pixies and the animate Celts.
There is no such thing as a sacred round dance.
But I lost valuable time hunting for lice in my pubis.
All around me people were dancing.
Of course, in the center, there is no motion.
But outside, the circle rotates, hand-clapping vibrates,
The sound of foot-stomping resonates,
And people smile.
People smile though the baring of teeth is a grin.
The animalistic evolutionary history of man is misleading.
From around the edge of the circle the isolates gaze on.
Inside the circle weaves, as the flower, diurnally.
Inside our feet come together in symmetrical pairs.
Inside we circle with neither clock nor escapement.
We are keeping time.

Inside, we are keeping time.
Oh, God, blues, jazz and rock and roll.
A girl says: Jesus Christ
And shakes her soul.

HOUSTON

I try to think about Houston White
I don't know if he's alive or dead
But I last saw him in Chaguaramas Bay
Leaning through the window of a car
And saying good-bye.

I couldn't talk then
Or to Coy Hendricks either
When he left the galley
With flour on his hands
To say good-bye.

Or to Mack MacMan
Who put his arms around me
When he was drunk
And wept about his life.
He said good-bye forever.

It was really forever
Although that bay
Still curves beneath the monkey mountains
Near the dragon's mouth.
It was blue in Venezuela
Miles away.

Good shipmates
Bad men,
Drunk forever
Who talked
When I was shy of speech
And couldn't breathe.

I was shy of speaking
About how much I needed them:
Bad men who talked.
They worked on rock piles
In the south,
Like fathers who went away.

THE NAME

I go into my shrink's office carrying a brown paper bag.
No one knows I am there except the man on the corner

I sit down with the bag on my lap, facing the window.
She asks me what I have in the bag, but I remain silent.

Instead, I open the bag. Nothing comes out.
I turn it upside down. Nothing comes out.
I turn it inside out. Nothing falls out.
I shake it vigorously. There's nothing in it.
I crumple the bag. Nothing pops.
I tear the bag down the seam and spread it out flat.
It's perfectly smooth. I ask her for a pencil.
I ask her for a book. Resting the paper on the book I write:
My name is Allen, find me.
I refold the bag and seal the seam with Scotch tape
         open the door and leave.
I hand the bag to the man on the corner. He begins to weep.
Somewhere I have seen that man before. That morning.
He holds the bag to his face and wipes at the tears.

NEED

Can't sit, can't run, can't walk
Can't ride in a car without leaning out.
Can't stay or go
Can't walk past a bar without going in.
Fishes off a trot line
Dives in the bay
Comes up with warm water on his back.
Screws on the beach at night
Hits the pimp boy in the mouth
Gets fighting drunk
And works the next morning.
Works the winch with gloves on
Paints the deck
Stands watch at sea
And drinks ten cups of coffee.
Talks, sings, tries to read the Bible
Thinks about revenge.
Spends years in prison
Drinks whisky
Never with the same woman twice.
Talks with the natives
Minds his own business
Runs off at the mouth.
Sits on the pier
Catches jackfish
Catches dolphin
Stabs the moored shark in the back.
Wears a black patch on his left eye.
Goes to the top of the mountain
And drinks beer.
Waits for his pimp to appear.
Never tells a lie.

Never tells a lie
Won't tell one
Can't tell one
Talks about his life.
Baptist preacher for a grandfather
Divorced from his wife.
Talks about his life,
Talks about wanting to be good.
Gets angry sometimes
Wants to hit
Wants to run
Wants hot chili on his food.

Wants hot chili on his food
Wants not to be alone.
Wants to have me for a friend
But I'm always alone.

I'm always alone
Can't talk for long
Can't keep a straight face.
Always lying
Always leaving
And I leave without a trace.

I leave
No good-bye
And I never come back.

Twelve years later
I think about him
My shipmate Mack

THE CAMEL

The camel's a beast has no need of a priest,
*   a professor or expert in trumping*
A failure at cards, religion or shards
He beats all at the challenge of humping

PAY-BACK

If I speak to you, the blind forces of comparison
*   hold me by the hair*
Like those Furies who throttled Orestes for killing the
*   blind bitch Clytemnestra*
Although no myth has it she was blind except my own
But when she and Aegisthos killed the king
She fumbled for his throat under the net
Not knowing who it was except by direction of
*   assistant murderers*
And when her own son paid her back with a thrust
*   through the mouth*
They tried to spread-eagle him, those black birds,
For ripping what was rightly dead
If I am not a murderer, then you see her perfectly.

THE YOUNG AMERICAN BUDDHISTS

The young American Buddhists
Are not rice bags
Are not saki jugs
As thin as farmers or court chamberlains
They march with cymbals and bells
With conches and ankle bracelets
But their shaven heads are so large
Thin, but so extraordinarily large

HOUSES

In Cancer the crab sneaks homeward —
Scipio Scipionis the fish;
In Leo the lion bites his ass;
Aquarius the servant breaks a dish;
Myron the Archer pulls a bowstring;
Sagittarius cries for his bow;
Cassandra the queen sets in winter;
Orion the hunter sets below;
The stars are incensed with one another;
It's crazy to look up and wish,
Better to keep your head covered
And watch from the ground while they spin,
Leo the lion has trouble with
Keeping his mangy fur in.

A SERIOUS QUESTION

Quite honestly,
Is it a fault to be so serious.
I get overwhelmed with my own feeling,
Like a resonant brick,
And then, I can't keep my place in the façade.
Buildings can't be made of bricks like that.
Bricks have to be rock steady,
And that they get from shifting around in a funny way.
But I'm dead serious,
And so I always shake,
While the others sway.
Even now.
I can't keep from being serious
What I want to say is:
I want to be alive.

Therefore, I may have to give up my part in the structure.
I may have to fall out altogether.
How long does it take a single brick to weather,
A reasoning, sentient brick?
I may lie broken in two, or three or four
Forever.
And live bricks die.
This isn't just whimsy,
It's a serious question.
Will I die?

ANKOU

Papa's come in from the fields with a fork on his shoulder,
Mama's climbing the haystack in search of the hens
And all the children home from their homes in the ground
Are new potatoes tumbling into the bins.
Ankou on his white horse, skinny as ever
Spins his head on his neck like a lighthouse light.
Dad with a grin is inviting him in for supper,
He must be gone before the beginning of night
        with Dad behind him.
Dead all right.

MY FATHER'S MUSTACHE

Back in the thirties my father grew a mustache
And he with his small and somehow soft brown eyes
His small regular features and wavy black hair could have been
The Turkish officer who slaughtered the English
          in the Dardanelles
Or the cavalryman who skewered the Bosnians at Sarajevo,
So economical was his rage and his fine coordination
So treasured up and finely dealt when it burst
          through his eyes.

His tears were extraordinarily large when he wept with rage.
Fine, hot and milky like the form and color of his hands,
And when he slammed teacups through a pane of glass
The little finger bent upward slightly.
It was the mustache of a warrior, that is to say,
          a murderer
Who finds his scope too small in war.

And now when I see the rim of a glass and the small
          suppressed creature that streaks around its
          curled edge when I move past it,
I imagine my father's soul, compressed there,
Small-eyed, angry, quick and murderous.

A RAY OF SUNLIGHT STRUCK

A ray of sunlight struck
The face of a corpse
The woods
A frog's face
The exposed nerve of a dying hare
The jacket of a copper slug   .
The exposed bud of a March tree
The face of a corpse
The sole of his boot
The cloud drifting over his face
The moon

NUDE WITH A TRUMPET

My friend in the bath house
Took her trumpet from its black case
And blew a long silver note that fell on the stones
Glistening with a kind of afterbirth
That died a long way off in the black spruce forest
And the creature which had just been born
Licked itself on the wet flags
And rose, following.
The quivering trees.

THE NAME LUZ DE ANDRADE

The name Luz de Andrade,
In the dawn off the island of Siau
Around the world and a hundred and twenty degrees west of
            the line of demarcation
In the year fifteen twenty-eight
Was carved in the husk of a coconut
By an almost illiterate seaman
From Oporto
Having carried a memory around the world —
How strange that so light a thing
Had not been blown before the wind.

I can see only the harbor
Glistening at the sides of the green-ridden caravel
And what that dark eye sees.
The name Luz de Andrade
How strange that so light a thing
Had not been blown before the wind.
Careened in a harbor,
The ship has a woman's belly shape.
The clouds hang down like tits
Above the metallic trees.
The water so flat
That a face can almost be seen
A fathom below its depths.
The chain runs into the sea and bends.
How strange that so light a thing
Had not been blown before the wind.
The name Luz de Andrade.

THE WELL OF DE SITTER

In the universe of De Sitter
There is a well deeper than the sun
Deeper than mind, deeper than the coil of life
And yet the distance from ocular to eye
Is only the moist distance of a summer well
To a face that shines into it on an afternoon;
Cool and not so deep
One sees the reflection of a star in the middle
          surface of the pool.
That never moves,
Not even the soft touch of pollen
Ever deforms that perfect surface
And the star.
Around the well is a meadow,
A quiet forest ticks against the ground.
The green surface of a canopy of grass
Flattens under footfalls.
Midges cling to their enormous toadstools.
Water from the previous rain
Fills with larvae.
Nothing touches or deforms
The sterile glistening pool in the well.
It is a membrane.
The quiet meadow.

IT WAS DEAD, IT WAS DEATH

For Wilfred Owen

It was dead, it was death
It was the resolution of dreams —
It was the composite of the water-picture
As when the soldier lies face down in death
And the sky mirrors,
And the water dries and breeds —
It was a poet named Owen, fifty years ago
Now dead, now with his head between his knees
Now choking with the dust of death
I saw beside the shattered copse of trees
More real than I am now
Weeping with my own dry tears
As I weep with his,
Until I strike the attitude of death
Not knowing whose it is
Or whom I please,
And carry back the fortune of the dream,
Poor pack, those hopeless psalmodies.

MY UNCLE FRITZ

My uncle Fritz came from Spandau
He was tall and blond and had muscles like giant
hard potatoes
And a perfectly rectangular face.

My uncle Arthur came from Poland
He was five foot three and weighed a hundred
and eighty pounds,
Perfectly square and hard as bone.

My grandmother Mollie came from the square family
of flatlanders
And her head, too, was perfectly square.

But my father was finely built and as slim as Enver Pasha.
He had Turkish blood in his veins.
Dark, quick, wirelike and insane.
He was much crueler than any of them,
A resentful fire burning in his dark eyes.
A dark insect with a sting.
His anger was as polished as a spider's carapace.

My mother was soft and round and blue-eyed.
Eastern Europe.
Prussia, Poland, Rumania
Twisting in and out of the Hunnish Varangian line.
A land of slaves and Jews and German colonists.
And peasant witches,
Square potato fields, vomit and blood.
My great-grandfather was a fur trapper.
A gnome dressed in sheepskin and felt boots.

All of them buried in a landslide of mud
And swallowed ferocity.

Not one of them worth a damn to anyone.
Not one of them with a crow's worth of joy.

SELF SERVICE (SELF PORTRAIT)

Around me
My typewriter
My friends
A book on the Russian Revolution
The moon
And a streetlamp with its mercury vapor
Rolling weakly along the street like fog.
In my head is a graveyard
With a wooden shovel streaked with mud.
My mouth hangs half open.
No flies fly in.

POINT OF VIEW

If only to take a point of view
The poet should undertake cabbagehood
And become a member of the mustard family
If not the family of man
Spreading, but concentrically, in the August Sun
He can bashfully hide the sweetness of his inner core
Behind the parasol of his outer leaves
Green and honest

FRIENDS IN A LANDSCAPE

For Bob Gross

I, from the outside, am a small bearded man,
And you are a larger one,
And both of us in a landscape painted, say,
          by Ma the painter
Might appear as two inconspicuous specks in the folding
          of a mountain ridge,
Above the pines and yet below an almost solid wreath of
          mist that hovers at the wind-safe side of the mountain
Seemingly at rest, yet obviously climbing, taking breath
          at an interval between two enormous climbs,
Taking the ridge ahead with a view of the land beyond
          not yet in sight,
Two friends in a not unfriendly scene which hasn't got the
          time or sentience to be aware of us —
It is so large and purposeful, with its pines, and birds
          and stone flesh
Moving under a moving sky.

I, from the outside, am a small bearded man,
And you are a larger one,
And yet we have the freedom of the ridge,
In this mountain landscape.

AMAGANSETT

I come out here—
The road, not yet archaic,
Turns in the scrub like a fading Cheshire lane.

I don't know who these people are
But they know me—
Now the worst of it comes from the woods.

To have a second growth,
So motley, shameful, pale
Is like the half-formed word of a bridled contempt.

There is no forcing here,
As in the sea wind
That covers the white backs of the summer weeds.

Only a road,
And the private, pale developments
of an elder dread.

And yet tonight
As the sea rises, as the moon rises
As the planets rise above the sea

There will be no sky
No trees of an elder dread—
The butterflies asleep.

We'll go naked and swim
From the sand bottom
To the moon, like babies.

DRUNK AT LAST

He looked like he'd been socked with a ball-peen hammer
Like the face of the moon all hammered in with the flat
end of the sickle
And rogered by the ham bone of an ox shingled with twenty
sheaves of iron scales
Bestialized by love
And given over to the first inmate of the first wardens'
school available
And that under bond by material witness,
In short, hamstrung, bound over tremble cocked
Sublimely pissed out and washed up on the beach
With a grain of eye in his modicum
Afloat and awash in boiler plates of moon
And drunk all over like the shingle of a starry scene
Better and better,
Tangled like the legs of an octopus
Reeking like a bar
Walking on the waters of love,
Ever living Jesus of the popular song,
Oh God, and hungry,
Walking between the hulls of the bay and the black
pier-side jump
Of the cable side moon, black cane jungle monkey island
darkness of Chaguaramas, Port of Spain—
And entirely alone
Except for the first tooth
And the black whine of the water

DOWN TO THE BEACH

Down to the beach for a party—
Salamanders, crows and a rail,
Birds get pebbles to swallow
Lizards get sand on the tail

Hugging and kissing between species,
Toes, legs and feathers fly—
Swallowing crows salamander
Feels that his throat's getting dry

Goes to the edge of the water,
Drinks a drink from the sea—
Down from his lips like a letter
A black feather droops obviously

But the rail goes down to the seashore
Walks by himself in the dusk—
The sun goes down in the water
Leaving an evening husk

Stars come out near the zenith
Yellow and spread down the sky—
Stoop-shouldered, long-legged and lonely
Rail is beginning to cry

His tears fall into the water,
The water licks at the shore—
The pebbles shift with the current
From where they were lying before

Rail walks back from the water
Holding a fish in his mouth—
Moon climbs up the horizon
Sailing full sail for the south

WITNESS

A quaint historical twist
Lincoln's ass-hole as the great backwoodsman lays a turd
In the White House privy
And the sound of good beef hitting the dead-fall sod
A sculptor forming Washington's finger up his nose and
Jack slaying the giant by swinging on his balls
The Washington Monument chipped into the shape of the
              penis that it is
And rammed into the Navy buildings on the Mall
As the marble horror of the Supreme Court staggers
              into the moat.
The President of the United States changing Thomas
              Jefferson's diaper
While Franklin Pierce, the falling general, falls
              dead drunk from his horse.
The United States Bank hemorrhaging greenbacks and
              fifty cent notes.
A march up Pennsylvania Avenue. The statues of the
              Ancestors in the Capitol.
The well of the Senate filled with water and great
              heavy silver carp.
The rotunda filled with monkeys and tropical birds.
The emperor of the United States trapped by fire and
              a riot of the blues and greens.
The ground giving way. The amortization of the national debt.
The siege, the fire, the saving of the coronation jewels.
Mistra as the Turks trap Michael Paleologus.
Recent scenes of slaughter in Dupont Circle.
The rage of the innocents and the impotents.
Claudius watching the sailors drown.
Washington winters. The blacks washing their cars
              on Sunday afternoons.
The mons veneris where the monument is.
Three hundred crazed radicals. A horse brigade.
All of this filled into a ditch ten thousand years old.

Who are we kidding. The moon is dead.
But the moon will circle the earth for
          a hundred million years,
Always showing the same face. For God's sake take pity
          on the children that you kill.
I am a witness and I say they are innocent. No one can rub
          the scratching from the moon.
No one can change this monument that holds a dead white face.
Washington, the Capitol, and a full moon in February. Witness.

BOXING AND WRESTLING

Boxing and wrestling are the sports of the underworld.
There, on the Acheronian plain, the dead athletes' agon
Raises clouds of gray dust
Which fulminates in the pale light of the undermoon.
The struggling corpses are covered with an odorless dew,
Sweating as they die.
No olive here provides the rub-down oil.

Boxing removes the face
As nailed fists swipe in sluggish arcs of enormous power,
As half a cheek rips by to reveal the teeth
And noses hang below a gaping cavity.
No fists are wrapped
Or mouthpieces soaked in vinegar,
And worst of all there is no ring of lookers-on.

Wrestling dislocates the heart.
The dead wrestle to exhaustion
Wrenching their lungs and guts with the strain of
            centuries without rest
And here all holds illegal under the sun are allowed,
Strangling, choking, arms across the neck
Full Nelsons, and the hauling backward of heads
            by the jaw
Until the neck-bones crack.

Boxing and wrestling, and then the Pancratium,
The free-for-all of ghosts who still possess their flesh
Unlike those others who, stripped naked, wail against
            the night.
Kicking in the groin, gouging, scratching with nails
Twisting and pulling of joints, the breaking of fingers
And the larger limbs.
And worst of all there is no ring of lookers-on.

ONE INFINITY

The Chinese had their cycles of time
But they were drunk
And were passionate
And had no use for anything that could not make a snake sleep
Or resound with the moon
Or grow in a field.
Even mountains can grow in a field.
But now also they built linear moments,

Clocks and escapements which measured the brilliance of
the preceding and following seasons
As in the school of Mo Ti
Who researched the field of cause and effect
And was forgotten in later times.
The lesson then from this is man's forgetfulness
His ability to reabsorb the history of his race
In a tiny rice flower.
All things flower
All things grow
And then, in transparency of decay they grow again.
Here forgetting and remembering is in
A tiny bowl of crackled glaze and clay.
It will break.
Here is my hand. Here is my love.
It will break.
Here is a tenderness of wisdom.
It will break.
Here is blood and water.
They will break
When the sea breaks and falls.
Now here am I.
Touch me.
Cross my heart with your hand,
I will not break.

MYTHFALL

Walking in the garden
Walking heavily
God set down his foot-fall
Beside the heavy tree
And darkness cast his shadow
From heaven commonly

No shadow now remains,
That is, no dreaming seems
In solid planes

No shadow now requires
The light of common fires
Or common flames

No garden grows the same,
Or feeds the same desires,
Or scratches with its briars
The heavenly knee.

JUST SIMPLY

Just simply how I love you
How I love, the red, the shy redness of your carapace
That shines from underneath the workmanlike
           darkness of your skin
And the segments, busy segments, of your threefold body
As it hurries across the page that I hold to the earth,
To the earth, to the cool dark earth
Beneath these flowing pine trees, in the shadows.

OR KEEP THEM OPEN ...

Watch out, I'm going to kiss you now,
Close your eyes, close them,
Or keep them open, that's all right,
I like to see your eyes until the moment
          when I kiss you
And then I close mine,
Brown, soft, I like to watch them roll
          beneath their lids
As your body leans softly against mine

THE POEMS

The poems stand on their heads,
The poems grin
The poems play in the breeze
As lightning approaches from the west
And when they drink water
They spray each other's faces with their mouths

The poems are not exactly children
Very often they have six feet or even more
And when they run it's more like a leaf tumbling
Except they sometimes know their way

Often in the darkness of a summer storm
They gather beneath the branches of a giant oak
And thumb their noses at the clouds
Since he protects them from the rain

But often they gather together after nightfall
Afraid of the dark
And they tell blind and foolish stories
Without rhyme or reason

Their main talent is for playfulness
And for hope
Since even when they make their grimmest faces
They're not as serious as the clouds
Or the ponderous, bulging earth,
And after all, they're only youngsters yet.

DREAMS

Dreams in rank of order,
First the greatest nightmares,
Pillar-sided and gray, with eyes, lashless and lidless,
Circling their conical heads
As tall as the buttressed gray oak
Smelling of the signaling piss of wolves
And the cyanine acridness of mistletoe,
The bottomless forest of an empty and solemn luxuriousness,
With its moving, ponderous forms
And the lacy ribs of decayed leaves . . .
Dreams of the first order . . .

And next the demimonde of dreams,
Brown bare devils with yellow teeth
And slit mouths grinning from the backs of their heads;
Their faces are blank and they look backward as they go
Into the past,
Their round eyes shining like skulls or stars
              until they disappear
Into a closet of webs
And the gray dust covers them up to the tops of their heads
And the muffled sound of their breathing sings
              from underground
Like the humming of moles . . .
Dreams of the second order . . .

And finally the third and smallest rank
Of tiny puff-cheeked women
Circling the woods with baskets made of twine and sticks
Rustling in the fall of last year's leaves for nuts
And dried insects
And bee turds and mounds of limey droppings from the nests
Which they mix at home with their bread,
And the shuffling sound of their feet is something
              like the sea

Which sounds so far away, so distantly
On the white shore,
And these are the dreams of the third order . . .

And now,
As I move through these woods
I see in the white starlight of the breakers
The white flanks of those without skins,
Playing in the moonlight,
As I dream and close my eyes
And perhaps this dream is not awake
Or the woods are dreaming
So far away, so distantly . . .

IN A SQUARE PATCH OF LAND

In a square patch of land the crows shot crap
In a little wood between two cliffs of land
Trees smoked up in March and died in fall
Chickadees played marbles with the wind
And games in all the hollows of the trees
Were played to by the sawyer beetle band:
The grouse beat hollow drumming with their wings
The birch got drunk until he couldn't stand:

It was a carnival, it was a township, it was a county fair
It was a place where all the actions were;
Fucking, fighting, wrestling on the grass
But all in fun: a fond perpetual mass

Winter seasons went and summer came
And with each season came its seasonal game,
Skating, sliding, swimming under ice
Eating seeds and cleaning fur for mice
Sliding down the banisters of streams
Climbing tulip trees in relay teams
And scratching grubs or lice

That was the land of the wood
That was where a stand of hemlock stood
Darkening the hillside with a green shade
As passionate as the gorge the river made.
That was the place where the blackbird sailed himself
Across the brown-backed dashing river shelf.
That was the place where the muskrat dug his hole.
In drier land the muskrat was a mole.

Not strangely enough the animals played with death
As if it were a game to lose one's breath,
Not strangely enough the animals played with sleep
As if it were a hillside gently steep.
The animal's affection was their game
And nothing was a hurt or had a name.
Nothing could laugh or weep.

That was a place that really was.
That was a place that was good without ourselves.
That was ourselves.
That was.

And now I float down a country road.
Effortlessly I go between tall birch trees.
The gray birch of the woods turns yellow and dies.
In the spring the life will rise
And spring form its winter thickening.

And I go between the trees
Light and afraid.
I am so small here
That nothing will threaten or upbraid.
Autumn is bright and clear

NURSERY SONG

All trees that I've known
Not one grew green
All children touched
Have fallen into dust
As flowers
In an evening
Of distrust

Though yet when stroked
They might spread and shower
Seeds on the ground
For birds to devour
As flowers
In a day
Of ripening musk

All offices of guilt
Have lately been filled
All gardens of trouble
Not left to grow wild
Are brown
And rotten
With child

And yet I have seen
Woods in expanse
Green and upgrowing
Wild and immense
In sunlight
Bird filled
And dense

And yet I have seen
Woods in the night
Lightly devoured
By level starlight
And
Secret
Delight

THE NURSE

The nurse hands me a letter addressed to
Validiva 110.
My companion is the Angel Sotiris
Of the land of the dead.

On the lawn the nurses sip tea,
And the dead too are dressed as nurses.

Above, the Great House rises in swathes of road.
Nothing is allowed to enter this sadness with me.

AN IGNORANT HISTORY OF INDIA

An ignorant history of India
Showing the Mogul invasion run backward
To the laying down of the first sedimentation
And all without prior knowledge of the existence of India
And all without showing at all
Any prior knowledge of sunset or evening
Large crickets flying in the faces of cattle
As they browse through a spiny grass
And the black chert percolating downward through
metamorphic rock

An ignorant history of China
Showing the men of Han
Biting their way through the sandstorms of Turkestan
Only to be stopped by a waving banner of demons
And then buried beneath tons of snow
And how this deposition does not last through autumn
And how their bones drift as white as the snow,
All summer long

All this is like a history of a man
Whose unknown country is more stratified than earth
And more mythologized than any India
Whose dreams are ritual
And whose thoughts are a brazen geology of sleep

O William Blake, humorless man,
You were right but dreary to write this history
Of demon countries:
God scratching his ass like an ignorant,
malicious boy.

THE TROUBLE WITH THE STORY I'M TELLING

Here is a man who travels into the future.
Once there he discovers that everything in
*   the world is alive.*
The inanimate has ceased to exist
And even the parts of his body talk together
Debating endlessly whether to break apart
Or stay together for a little while longer.
But at this point I can't seem to go on any further
The story leaves me and travels alone
To a place in the future I can't reach or see
Because my dreams haven't covered that distance yet,
Or because I'm afraid to follow them.
Either way the story remains unfinished.
And for some reason, this is the part of the story
When my time traveler also finds himself alone,
Abandoned by his only two companions in the world.
He is walking through a field of flowers which bend
Away from his step. Leaves curiously brush his face.
Clouds follow him overhead, playing their shadows
Over him like nets. And then he disappears
Into the dense white growth of the page.
His description is unavailable
But I have followed his track into the ground.
It ends there, with the world playing around him
While he clutches a sachel full of stolen
*   money to his chest.*

BUSINESSMAN'S WAR

That shield which Achilles holds against the ground
        looks like a bicycle wheel
And that throwing stick of Ajax seems a greasy spanner
        used for tightening chariots
And also Diomedes' wand more like a flashlight that prowling the
        outworks would be useful for
Than a thyrsus wet and dewy from a heifer's cunt-hole
Or a captured Aethipian commander's mace—
Where could we see a face as shifty as Ulysses' in a lowdown bar
And where an arrogant muzzle like Menelaus except in some
        court of law,
In fact the whole prospectus of the Trojan War
Should have been a week in Asia Minor,
With heat laid on by sunlight, orgies for the shade,
And swimming in the sea enforced by Trojan infantry,
A cycling tour, and a stirring night parade,
Or what is advertising for? What could be finer?

Ever expect full value for what you've paid?

MURDERED WAR

Murdered war sat on the stairs
Eating apple pie
And wondering.

I thought the world was shaking
The houses and the streets
Were all in one resonant beam
Vibrating between the sun and the core of earth

And the room where I sat
Was also trembling
And following—
Wall by floor by canopy

Murdered war,
Self-murdered beast with one hand
Eating and wondering
In fine consideration
The dropped stars of his artificial mouth.

His thoughts were plaster
And dried blood,
His buttocks were brown
And callused as great trees
From sitting there so long.

And stars that weren't real
Dropped from the corners of his mouth,
Setting fire to his wooden thighs,
As he rocked himself to sleep.

ENDLESS SHOALS

Skimming over the lake of sighs in his glass-bottomed coffin
Coleridge woke periodically to write his dream
Drawing up his rope from Endless Shoals
He let the wind take his drenched sheet and carry him on
Not pressing the water more stridently than a water walker
He listened to the Delphic chorus of fish
Bellowing the chorus of a future opera
Was it Coleridge or an Angel who accepted a kiss?

At the bottom of the lake the peasants built a cathedral
Drawing itself away from the dome by the shore
Blood-red sandstones and iron angles
A sea-green vault and a nave invaded by silt
There Gogol had to attend the funeral
Of a witch with green eyelids and scale black hair
Keeping himself apart in a bathyscaphe
He ventured out in helmet and canvas gloves

But along came the hordes of the water walkers
Sweeping from end to end of the church in a wave
Knocking the paintings askew and scaring Madonna
Knocking her down and floating away with her fetus
Jesus Christ was eaten by fish as a baby
The second is an imposter changed by the trows
Neither one was a savior by the end of the day
And Coleridge went on, pulling his arm bone sculls

She too had her own coffin to pull in
But he forgot her when he woke to remember his dream
Riteless and dirgeless she skimmed the lake in a fury
Sometimes above water sometimes under the surface
Shooting into the sky she became a constellation
Of four square stars on a sunrise yellow ground
And Gogol trudged kicking the silt at the bottom
Looking for boughs of laurel buried and drowned
Coleridge went on, pulling his arm bone sculls
But he never said crack when the sun-risen witch said whip
But he never said drown when the sun-risen witch said die

THE CANNIBAL'S HELPER

First she commits seppuku
By stabbing herself in the stomach
And then without ripping up
And spilling out her guts
She follows me into the kitchen
Where I've heated up the stove:
All ready to roast her body when she dies.
But she's not dead,
She only follows me around the house
With a smirk on her face
And a small neat elliptical incision in her belly.
She wants to embrace me
Thinking to overcome me by the force of my aversion.
But I surprise her by taking her shoulders in my hands
And holding her close.
She's not even very bloody
But I can't remember whether her body is warm or cold.
I could have eaten her then,
Neither dead nor alive.

FIFTY OR MORE

I am your brother
And some events are simultaneous
In some frame of reference.
My friend sleeps in the next room.
The moon and the sun are in the same binding sheet.
Plaits of garlands are in the hair of Ramses
Existence is no predicate.
Kant sleeps underneath a white stone.
Darwin in positive strolls across the tundra.
The dew of the tundra quivers on the boot-tops of the drover.
A billion years from now the moon will be small and white
        in a clear empty sky.
All of this impossible predicate happens at one time.
My friend sleeps in the next room.
Those whom I know I count to fifty.
The midnight traffic passes along a street laid along
        the back of the moon.
All my friends sleep:
Sue dreaming in twists and houndings,
Robert tunneling through a brass tube,
Joan rushing between trees,
Mark whistling in a rough wind,
Margo watching a tidal wave at her feet,
Carol edging between walls that lean over,
Julie passing in and out of magic baths,
Joe sailing over a forest of scissors,
Sidney washing his eyes in a bath of brown umber,
Fifty in all we sleep under the same moon.
That small white predicate.
And if you know no predicates you hold your pillows against
        your cheeks like children,
You turn and cough and crease your bed sheets
Your mouths fill with water
Your feet run like hunters

You rumble and groan and grip the air above your
             mountainous beds
And you turn and hold your pillows against your cheeks again,
And sleep like children.
I am awake for you.
I smooth your hair and I wipe your flowing lips.

IT'S STRANGE

It's strange whom I get off with:
Lions, goats, the latest choice in fire hydrants
The mute piece of a banjo found in a bear trap.
Thing, animal, girl, boy
Number three pencil, a roll of transparent tape
All of these I've managed to spend one night with
In the last six months.
My bed has been rumpled a thousand different ways
And even a rather large camel fell through
To the next apartment on his hump.
Once I found myself fucking with my own manuscript
Which insisted on getting on top.
There's nothing in the latest manuals that offers guidance
On foreplay with an ashtray.
I've even fucked with myself
And found me hard to warm up.
Those I like best are a harem of female light bulbs
Hooked up in series
And a cage full of dragonfly nymphs.
Often I lie back and watch them perform together
While I stroke the backs of my favorite pubic lice.
Tonight's the night with my friend Sir Michael Mouse
But tomorrow I'll be in his girl friend's paradise.

THIS MORNING

This morning I shat small turds like a rabbit,
Yesterday I met your dead grandmother
At a dark moonless crossroads—
My image in the mirror is still harelike but human
Don't be afraid of ghosts
They can't transform you
Into a hare
Or a smile with teeth

I met your grandmother
At a crossroads of string
When I untied the package
Her world flew apart

PART OF MY FACE

What does it matter,
You're still part of my face.
Are you my nose, eyes or mouth?
Are you the cheeks, the facial planes
The straight temple
Or an ear convolved with traps for sound?
Are you the look of my mouth
When I speak or chew
Or are you the chin I touch
When I think and lose my thought?
You are some part of me
And yet one thought of losing you
Sees

Without being seen
The massed courage of a hill
In the headstrong light of the sun
That levels in a late August evening

Like the barrel of a gun.
The trees are thick
Their green is yellow green,
The pin oak, the white oak
The basswood and the maple tree,
All burning,
In the wind from the west,
Gathering light even from death,
And growing.

BOURBON

A glass of clouded Jack Daniels
Stands on my bedside shelf
And I wonder what kind of organism lives
In ninety proof bourbon
That makes it turn so milky brown
When I leave it there for several days
To make my room drunk instead of me.

Or for that matter,
What voyaging rotifer or crab
Drifts through the sequenced room of the air
Unseen by me
And lands on my radio, my coverlet
My lamp?
Would it be, that tiny monster,
An adjunct of my personality I cannot see?

It seems that if
Jack Daniels can support life
Then why not my bed, my clothes,
Or a false thought
Unconsciously nutrifying the environment
With a speculum of real dreams?
Does it seem unlikely that I am part of space?

Am I really then
Not so inhospitable to life,
Or rather no different from the black soil
That smears between my fingernails
A glaze of green?
Am I an oasis
In a desert of aerial embarrassment?

These questions,
Impostulations of a false philosophy,
Are nonetheless the food of minds
Which have the cells of the mind for subject,
The end of the nose for object,
And the top of the head as a platform
On which to gaze at the feet.
Nothing can be more certain than the self-deluding image of mind,
Or less so for that matter.
Paradox is the muse
Of undusted rooms.

Meanwhile I see the slow evaporation of my booze,
And I wonder if getting shit-faced is worth it any longer.
Perhaps I should just grin
As I did the other day
When space moved in
And found another friend in me
Willing to share my bed with a needy parasite
Or the Rome apple of sunrise.
Anything with friends
Cannot be lying there undrunk, if

Red and fiery turns white
And then the night,
or sunset either

POONTANG BLUES

With respects to Ed Field

Tom Isbrandsen,
Who wrote the poontang blues
Was up late again last night
Trying to think of a new story
To make up for the deadline on Tuesday morning
But he couldn't think of anything deadly enough
To write for the Daily Inquirer
And so he went to sleep in an attempt to dream about monsters
Preferably female
Who would come to him in the middle of the night
And offer themselves to him,
Monstrous body and soul
For the rest of the night
And how he would laugh at them in horrified contempt
And hide his head under the pillow
The way he did when he was an adolescent
In Brilling, Montana,
Thinking of the girl at the drugstore who sold Day's Work
                chewing tobacco
And Red Man plug
But who now was probably married
With seven kids to take care of
But he lay awake dreaming about the Union Central railroad tracks
And saw each separate cinder of the ballast taking shape
As he traveled in his mind from coast to coast.
About three in the morning she finally came
Dreaming of him too
And walking in her sleep
Straight into his bedroom at Second Avenue and Eighty-Seventh
                Street
Warning him in a humming sleeping voice
Of the horrible revenge of the female id.

He had to admit to himself, even while sweating coldly
That she was the monster of his dreams
Of his dreams entirely
And also his fear personified.
It seemed to him that he was afraid of women
Even since his mother washed him in the sink
That time she ran cold water down his back and he screamed
When he was only eighteen months old,
And now he wondered why she'd looked so gleeful
And decided it must have been
Because she had a horrible masculine id of her own
Which came to haunt her dreams
And take her away to the land of the castle of Bluebeard.
But who ever heard of Bluebeard in Brilling, Montana.
It must have been an archetype
In his case
Haunting the family.
Those classes at the New School were really a great help.
And the next morning he finished his story
About a newly discovered tribe in New Guinea
Whose women all had three vaginae
And were insatiable
Thereby exhausting their men at an early age.
No one who was male lived beyond the age of thirty in that tribe.
He considered giving up women entirely but decided on revenge
            instead.
He tried to remember his father's way with women
His father was a blue-eyed handsome man who liked to go to
            the rodeo
And the stock show,
And wasn't afraid of women at all, he thought.
He would have loved the poontang blues
But one day he was caught up against a fence by a stud bull
And fucked to death.
His father had never had much education.
But he met his deadlines.

AMERICAN EPIGRAM

Locked in an embrace
Whether fond or not no one can tell
Since they never leave their room

Fucking or scratching
It's all the same to me
But I can see
At least they manage to eat well

I see them always
Eating together at dusk
Like animals
That come to the barn
When the farmer spreads his corn.

Sad, without lowing
Like the cows at dusk
They lower their sad heads.
And consume their meal.

ABANDONMENT

For Gregory Corso

I know what you mean, Gregory,
The shitty childhood
The sense of abandonment constantly hanging over your head
Like a rose with spikes
The emptiness
Except I was never abandoned like you were
In prison
With an empty father's gates lying open
To receive no guests
I always had a home in the literal sense
Although it was no more a real home than some shit-house
Abandoned on the beach at Pelham
By the national can company / And still
My father was a raging set of contradictions
Like boiled-over alphabet soup into which the cook spits
And my mother was a cipher that hadn't even been boiled yet
But who made me eat my half-digested vomit from the morning.
And still the rose hung over my head:
The phony prettiness of her smile
Which only she thought as pretty as a rose:
She was bent on proving that her anger sucked milk.
And now I lie about my past
Because they didn't have the guts to abandon me.
But I think about the beautiful boy I call my son,
And he's happier than you and I were, Gregory.
At four and a half he's almost as tough as you are,
        you sweet bastard.
At four and a half he can push away the vomit
Or smell the rose without fainting from fear.
At four and a half he's not mine anymore.

PANDELION

Pandelion, beautiful rose of the lion,
Going to bed with girls is not half so much fun
As stroking your lion-yellow mane
And listening to you purr gargantuanly
You ten-ton pussy-cat
You are the largest flower in the world
And your smell is strong even beyond stink
Or stench, you writhe with growing, and the sun
Follows you around the blue arena of the sky.
You are mine, you are my only pet
And you follow me by growing underground
With roots that stalk and lean from
Molehill, to passageway, to ant rook
In the ground beneath the woods. You disappear
And reappear in meadows miles apart, and when
You flower it's like the whole sun
Smiling at itself with a double image in the west
When you lean across the broad meadows
Your beams are parallel and powerful
A table of roses and crocuses and yellow lace,
Above them, stretching them into the sky.
You are the message that the followers of birds unwind,
A scroll of still night-wind in the shadows.
I water you with blood that's singular to my own.
I sing you to sleep
As you curl around the rock in the sky,
Snoring as that mountain sinks forever,
Growling in the mirror-watchful night,
Painting in the rose-red sky asleep.
You sleep, lion, with your mane
Held half-breath in the darkness

WHY I WRITE POETRY

A lot of times I used to see rats
Coming in through the windows.
A lot of times I also used to see
Myself an effeminate baby
Crying for words out of a drooling,
Lisping mouth. My father was there
Watching me in my crib
As he passed by with contemptuous aversion.
What was the purpose of the round-house
Swing he took? He always beat me to the punch
And then pulled back his hand, smiling
For the next and always blow, his demonstration
Of superiority. What did he get out of it,
So big and strong, except a kind of bitchy
Nothingness which drowned me brown? And
Later I saw in every male stare the same
Withdrawing punch, as if my hit were
Preordained,
And then, rats coming, drooling through
The window like tongues.

A lot of times I used to bubble the rats
In prisons and send them sailing away,
Over the meadows of gardens paved with rose leaves,
The American beauty, the special Eisenhower
Black bulb, the crocus of desire,
The deaf-mute pandelion which leaned against
The dry wind. I was fertilized, me, that
Garden, with staring flowers and their mates,
The awful ten-tailed rats of infinity.

And now, of course, I walk on two simple legs
Through the gardens of Christiansand, a
Northern port on the edge of the Norway Sea,
Or sometimes in the current of the warm-washed Mexico
Against the brown shark and the black umbrella tree.
I am simply alone.
Or then, with a friend, I have my arm around
Their company for a moment out of the wind
With my feet on solid ground.
Or paint the rose with a brush too wide
But still my own. It was those rats I used
Against themselves, and the punches I pulled, and
I walk, not on stumps, but on toes,
And barely.

THE BRASS BAT

I saw batman in the window
Like an emperor who's just discovered
He has crabs,
Destroying poems with
A golden breath of pigstink
As they fell from the windows of the mind
Outside the trees—
Norway maples
Japanese pine
Obligatory London planes
And hawthorn leaves
Just like the ginger jars of the Chinese.
Only batman
With his cape of blue crass fustian
And his skinny shanks
Could appropriately
Impersonate
The northwest wind
Without being noticed
By the campus police
Who are no better critics
Than anyone else
Confusing autumn
With a dog and fleas
In blue drag.

But then we pinned him
By one wing
To the windowsill
And asked him his name
While threatening him
With tannis leaves
And he said:

Please,
I'm just a poor
Honest justiciar of crime.
Molest me not.
And then he scratched his balls
With his left foot.
They tinkled.

I SAW DEATH

I saw death riding down Broadway on a white charger—
His face was tired and lined, a decrepit cavalier
And his horse was a skinny jade with hanging folds of skin
She could barely carry his skinny thighs
And her forelegs quivered when she took a step
I thought she was going to pitch him overboard
But his grip was still firm enough for her
And they lurched between the bicycles and the handcarts
And the 104 bus.
I went over and patted her neck; he stopped and looked down
            at me,
I asked him his name, he said Death
And with the last sibilant his mandibles cracked.

His mandibles cracked and he put them back in place
And his long white fingers caressed the knob on his chin.

Where are you going, my poor friend,
Where are you going, skinny death?
I'm riding north, he said,
With my last breath.
His occupits were sad and black
Deep and black.

I am almost dead, said Death,
I can barely ride,
Would you like to walk by my side?

I took his hand,
Held his cold hand in mine
While through his threadbare robe I could see
His curved white spine.

Turning my face to his I smiled
And squeezed his fingers—
His pace wasn't fast
His reflection passed in the windows along the street
One after the other:
Toy stores, couturiers
Bakeries, tax consultants
        A restaurant, a bar.
He swayed and shivered as if cold
The warm November sun seemed young.
Hooves clicked softly on the tar.

I had the interpretation of dreams by Freud
Under my arm.
He stopped once at a traffic light
And took it from me.
He opened to page 64
Where it said:
... for dreaming rises superior to time and space
And then he smiled and was dead.
I left his horse and body there.

I SEE MY FRIEND

I see my friend Delphin del Castillo
Sauntering down Eighty-seventh Street.
He wears Christ in a side-holster
And the Broadway bus runs over his shadow.
As quickly as nightfall
He dissolves the bus with a magic bullet.
He comes from Guayaquil
And his mission there is to convert the Jews.
His ancestors were Olmec Indians
And his round face gleams like a nephrite moon.
But here on Broadway
He accosts one bearded man after another
Thinking that all of them
May be agents of the rabbinate
And all of them as convertible as Numbers two and three,
Where Moses separated the sons of Aaron from the rest
Of the sons of Midian.
One of them has a herringbone stuck in his teeth.
None of them pay attention.
And yet, Delphin is a former third baseman
Who played for Castro in Cuba
And if you tell him to cut the goddamn shit
He will discuss the pivot play and the overshift.
Castro pulls the ball. Che leaned into it.

God is the truth, or how could he make the world?
Delphin plunges through waves, with his trigger finger curled,
Watching the damnation of the foolish Jews
With a calm horror, and singing hymns of salvation as
He scatters pamphlets above the Sanhedrin manholes.
He'd like to quit the religion game. And
Get past triple A ball. But
Christ only called him as far as Montreal.

He calls me by name and pats me on the back.
His smile is as beautiful as the moon of his face
And he likes to meet me here on winter afternoons.
I say Delphin, I'm not really a Jew, but he looks at my beard
And he rubs the testament on his hands like resin
Drying his palms on the dry testament of Paul.
O Delphin don't you see how beautiful life was?
I too played the game and put the wood on it all.
Let's forget to convince each other
It makes no difference to God or the sky
If I believe in your truth
Or you believe mine.
Let's go down to the park and sweat in the sun
And hit fungoes, whether God is three or just one.
Let's play happily all day, and then go home in the dark
And drink beer, which is truly God's work.
Let's be happy and hear the sound of leather on glove.
Let's laugh and slide into third, which is truly love.
Let's be comrades and teammates and play at the game
For though you believe in God, Delphin, he will love you the same.

MOVIE KING

So England has a schizophrenic king
He sees once more
All the ghosts of all the murdered men
And women, and cup-bearers, and hind-stalkers
Drifting out of the mist, the mindless
Manikins of trouble
Shaking knotty fingers of blenched oak
In his warring face
And he, a starved orphan of the family of power
Who has no more friends or even interested enemies
Must fight them off with a weak-as-water sword
Made up by the hanging masters of arras
For the royal hand of England to unwield
Until with shivering step they crowd
Into the small spaces of his prostate and his gut-hole
There to nibble him to death with hemorrhoids
And yellow discharges
Of Wales and England.
He dies by falling on a giant can-opener
Left over from the Earl of Shaftesbury's picnic.
He cries tears of Bovril
And dribbles Tenant's lager from his mouth.
He is the movie king of England
The monster of the stagey set,
And there, with credits at the end
He sweeps his tawny wig in pageboy style
Across the languishing arquebus.
What king is this
That England never won
Except in dreams of Kodak Morris dances
In Beverly Hills?
The Culver City cowboys rope his knights.
The heads of Griffith Park are gargoyles to his fall.

American king of England
Weeping and weaving across a stage of silver
Dancing across the pebbles of the silver stream
Like a giant humpbacked crayfish against the tide,
How do you come to be the mirror
In our western moralizing nut-house,
Sluing us with your hammy hick-straw image
To the faint reality of our own maximum elected governance?
In a diction blended of Stratford and Secaucus
You remind us of the ghosts that Harding must have cried
When laying down the straight flush of his heart
He saw the phantom of Albert Fall waving the four-aced hand
          of death
Across his mouth.
Your epicene slobber trails between the legs of your crooked
          house on K Street,
Drunk on a posset of Jack Daniels and branch water,
While the moist cunt of the Navy Department quivers helpless.
You are the painted corpse of all the Pentagonish viziers
Learned in the art of changing money into war
Whose conical caps erupt in spires from the moon.
You are a crazy wicked clown
We can laugh at, dying.

You are, in space
A time of no dimensions changing vigorously to death,
While the sun weeps tears of crude oil.

Then come, movie king,
Take us on the trippy road to the fairy tale
Where only monarchs of an older age tread war and torture
As the field of Agincourt was trod
And Tewkesbury, and Poitiers.
We have no politics we cannot shed
With time in thirty millimeters
And space in a can of film.

We will not speak about ourselves
And our denizens of defoliated Burnham
The forest cannot move in magic time of Hollywood,
Proud Duncan speak in movie magazines
With fantasies of elves,
Except as nightmare wills it
Deathtime sees it through!
Movie King, elder time,
You fit the deadly shoe of Death,
And we are you.

THE REAL DEVIL

The temptations of St. Anthony were in fact
A piece of bread and a goatskin full of water.
You'd be surprised what fancies are performed
With a piece of bread.
In the desert a skin of water
Is like a harem of a thousand girls.
The devil is stingy with his toys,
His weakness is his self-contempt
His black tail delicately curls.
He's got no feeling for exuberance
Even in self-denial,
Everything with the devil is slightly out of style.
But if he'd brought real girls
With cunts like flowers
The saints
Would have fallen off their towers
And buried their noses in the smell
Of real roses.
But saints are more demanding
They want the whole world to go down with them in error
Or rise upward singing in joy.
They're much less parsimonious
They're more human
Less understanding.

And so with access to unlimited wealth
The Devil kept it to himself
And offered bread and water
Worth then, in ases
A lousy quarter.
St. Anthony laughed.

AN ALPHABET

100 Etudes
Beginning with Ah
The syllable of the caves
Wind blowing Aeolus
Actor of weights and seasons
Feather spring and sharp bony February
Beppo
Beginner and Ender
Clown and ass-tail of a duck
Pom-pom and bunny button
Red spot and nose bulb
Cappo
Crier and creature
Of August Ravines
Sweaty, heavy and murderous
Grief-ripe and wicked
Daddo
Keeper of sheep
Big nosed, big horned and buttock strong
Rebounder of stones
And caller of hollow cries
Sheep head himself
Etta
Mountain of grape-vines
Shady, sun-strong
Purple at distance
Tufa gray at close range
Steep and porous soiled
Fragga
Black, sharp-winged raven
Red-beaked with entrail
Rock hidden, offal laired
Stick dwelling bird of crags
In Troll-fjord

Grotta
Oil black water of a pond
Holding nutritive secrets
For crayfish, carp
And great black frogs
With membranous, slimy skins
Halda
Land of wide valleys
Swept by a sun-bosom
From east to west,
Rich, red-soiled,
Grape and olive growing
Inga
Polar cavern of rich blue ice above the floes
Seal riddled
Skua ridden
Smelling of fish
Jakka
Sword of the palace guard in Heimland
Useful for lice bites and quick revenge in the straw
Below the king's palette.
Also the guard himself
Kroll
Hideout of mountain rebels
Folds in volcanic plugs impossible to search,
A labyrinth of a thousand ambushes
And kingdom of younger sons
Menda
Adviser of princes
Old and advised himself
By poverty enforced in youth
And wealth too late to enjoy
Noda
Horseback riding foul smelling
Prince of nomads
Horse eating also,
And cannibal in mid-career

Opar
Princedom of black forests,
Water spirits and mold white father ghosts
With long entangling hair
Poter
Wide sunny land of golden chateaux
Canals, fields and forests of oak,
But mean bitten, parsimonious folk
Querl,
Small south oceanic island
Of elephant seals and whaling stations,
Where oil reeks like a surf of dead life
Crashing on the stones
Redda,
Prince of a land of monasteries,
Where deviousness is treasure
And he is wealthy in looks and black, tight
Nimble stockings
Suda
King of equatorial currents,
Crab eater, copra shredder,
Fisher of coral beasts and
Warm current sailor
Troppa
Civilized
Warm cultured land of small towns,
Wine drinking, but under a shadow
In times yet to come
Unser
Bird of Pelagic cyclones
Never resting, stretching eyes to the wind
At the tips of its wings
Vactor,
Sloth of small latitude forest
Steamy furred as the jungle
Never resting at night
Slimy tongued

Wakka
Song of jungled, volcanic promontory,
Secret in ceremony, wooden idols
And red dye
Xinga
Instrument of inland equitoria
Wooden plated, resonant,
Woman voiced in song
Yek
Ox of the highlands,
Hairy nosed, bare-assed
With short front legs
Zeega
Overcoat made of camel wool,
Worn by the tribesmen in the cool uplands
And useful for its many pockets

A SOLID REGIMEN

A solid regimen of poetry
As well as fine Havana cigars for everyone
Even monkeys
And a bridge of bread over the Rhine
Dropping crumbs on the Niebelungs' gold
And an airy fairy rainbow
Busting the windows of the Chase Manhattan Bank
And a choir of poets standing around
In long black beards and brown homespun
Like Hatfields
Bellowing epics of dragonflies
Across the misty mountains
Now that's my idea
Of a good future
Not one of your mental mushroom
Ramp and spinoff futures
Whose only tweet comes from an unoiled
Computer spindle
And without any fairy tales at all—
Of course I think we can keep space
In our picture
But I'd like the spaceships to be
Hollowed-out Danish salamis
With fins made of rollmops
And if you think it can't be done
You have no faith in the future.
That's what we need—
Faith in a decent future to be crazy
Funny, lustful and gluttonous
But not cruel.
What if a few bankers cry
Like tiny tots at the waste of all that gold,
All those gilt-edged securities
They counted on to gentle them through old age,
We'll wipe their tears and give them

Hershey's kisses
And tell them to run along and play
In the fields of jack-yellow barley
And not to get their feet dry
And that banks are henceforward declared to be
Open zoos where cheetahs can roam at will.
And also we can tell all the misinformed policemen
That henceforward if they want to they can be
In charge of directing the mist to pull off the road
And also of preventing the sea breeze of leaving the right
Lane when it comes off the beach in the evening
And heads out to cool the brows of the sharks
And the leprelions
Who've had hot days thinking of pearl divers.
No, we'll not be cruel
But we're damn well going to have some fun
Whether some people like it or not:
Revolutionaries, rightists
Anarchists, fascists,
Functionaries
Bureaucrats, professors and contra-professors
Deans, executives, chairmen of the board
And filthy rich, also grumpy poor,
For everyone in the world, if they want it,
We'll have pretzels and beer,
But pretzels with all the mysterious curved beauty
Of a double twisted Moebius strip
And beer the color of the golden Rhine
When the Rhine Maidens used it for a sitz bath
And that's that,
Take it or leave it.
I hope they take it.
I wish they'd get off their horrible non-fun trip
And write some poetry.
Pretzels and mustard
Like in Philadelphia,
Only without Philadelphia.
And beer in golden tankards
Without the gold.

EMPTY SPACE

The beregini were those to whom ego left her eggs
And the white meat of the egg became the white skin
And the yellow yolk, the hair.

Young female spirits
You can see them gliding between the dry spikes of the marsh
On smoke instead of legs

Except all that was dead when ego died,
Only the mad and the very young can see them now
In odd corners of the room.

My young son too
One afternoon when he'd done a brave thing
Saw another boy walking by his side.

But I could not see whatever it was,
Although I walked there too and kept the pace—
The sun shone through empty space.

CONSIDER THE MYSTERIOUS WASP

She rises
And then she rises above the shore
Level sand, white sand
Stretches out
Like a table set before the sea
Which eats, and eats

She returns from the flowers,
The level-set bluebells and phlox
And finds her nest.

She carries in her mind
The set pattern of the grainy field
Of flowers.

She enters
Through a tunnel in the moist sand
And walks about her chamber.

In her mind
The flowers bloom
As she lays her eggs in the spider's flesh.

She is so beautiful
That even death is charming
And the sea is rhythm to her poetry.

And then she rises
She rises
In the cold sunlight of September
At the border of the North Sea shore
Glinting
Her filmy wings.

Mysterious wasp,
Alive
You are animate sand
Sea
Wind
And winter is the egg you lay
In the body of Spring.

Dead, you are a honeycomb
A carapace
And finally
Huge eyes in the flowering darkness.

I too am such a thing
And yet grieve
Unreasonably
For lost love.

There is no such thing in us
As love lays her eggs in us
As dying
In futility.
Level sand
Stretches out
Before the sea.
She returns from the flowers.

PROPHECY IN BRIDGEPORT

The main thing is
Let your limbs flow out
Arms splayed like the Bank of New York
With its fingers unclenched
Legs thrown out like the Wall Street Journal
With its cock draped downward in a curve over its balls
And let your head loll to one side
Drooling in the manner of Sikorsky helicopter
When its rotors fail
And so in this way
You must allow the fall of evening to penetrate you
To grind against the walls of accommodation
To sink more deeply toward the womb of your grief
As the gray March evening falls, relaxes against the ground
        of Bridgeport.

Let the Penn Central
Slide
Toward New York on the tilted table of Connecticut
Let the green canals slip on bearings toward
The duck farms of Long Island
Let the southern breezes blow
Across the brow of P. T. Barnum's grave.

Things must relax
The station fall apart
The shutters of the baggage claim droop
Those heavy eyelids fall across the racks of carpet bags
The fat policeman doze on beds of commercial waste
The bowling bar on State Street lean against
The cup for Polish strikes
The freighter from Virginia rust against the dock at Remington
The old saloon fall and sleep in a puddle of beer
On the porch of a rotting boardinghouse on Gregory Street

I know
That I know the dream on the mummy's face
Who sleeps in the Barnum museum on Main Street
And I know
That my redeemer rides the old red circus wagon
That once carried boots for Tom Thumb's funeral
And I know that
He is the man who curry-combed the red back
Of McLevy Hall,
When Lincoln spoke to the black-eyed abolitionists
And I know
That he is the man who laid manure
On the bed of Jumbo's grave.

Come back
Old mist
Come back
Old foggy gumbo of the salt marsh swamps
Come back
Mud of the bottoms near the shore
And white birds colored gray
By the late March smoke of burning clamshell fires,
Come back felt-helmeted policemen
Come back
Parades on Main Street
Tickling the shoulders of Bulgarian strong-men
Come back slanting white sunshine and swelled buds of April
Come back
Sleep of bums near the station
Ruffled by the wind of the 5:09
Come back
Stretched sleep of the flats of bitterns and rails
Come back
Flat may Long Island sound
Clean and filled with migrating sturgeon
Atlantic salmon
Whales and sea squid
Come back

Long life, long summers, long shadows
Come back
Long sleep in the laps of red hawthorn bushes and beach berries
Come back
Sprawling, innocent
Deer herds, flights of pigeons.

I see
Like cinders in the eyes of smokestacks
In the Casco paint factory
I see
Like specks of gristle in the casing of Roessler's hot dogs
The coming death
The coming death of reasons
The death
Of haircuts and barbershops
The cutting down of children's shadows
With axes of grief
I see coming
Over the rolling country farther north
From over New Haven
From over the elephant brows of New Hampshire
From over the bumpy dairy farms of lower Quebec
From over the black magmal shield of Newfoundland
I see coming
Coming,
Swift as the migrating geese of November
The shadows of the sunward falling shadows
I see
Human death
Village death
The deaths of factories
Families
Athletic contests
Softball teams
Atlantic lotteries
Numbers at lunch hour
Coffee in the parlor.

I see
The crumbling of patrol cars
The bones of children
The skulls of high school principals
Locked in mouthed embrace with the mandibles
Of the blind doughnut shop on John Street
I see
Fraternity pictures buried under tons of snow
I see
Locker rooms
Drifting like storms across the landscapes of the public library
I see
The Algonquin club grinning at the sky.

And I see change
And I dream change
Coming
Lying in my case
My tibia
My long bones lying on velvet.
I see
As the mummy sees
Long years
Coming swiftly southward like shadows
Migrating past the strongholds of dead men.

And I
Let my limbs flow out
They are tides
They are slow evenings
I let
Them nestle in my armpits
I let the power lines wrap my shoulders
I let
The diesel engines nestle my groin
They have no power
They sprout rain
They grow

Leaves and branches
They drape forward into summer
They loll sideways against November
They drool snow
Into the mouths of the beach palmettos
They drift against the flanks of sharks
That follow warm streams from the gulf between the legs of
        striding medusids.

And now
I let myself sleep.
Come over me
Futureless, humanless sun
And warm the drifting hollows of the pin oak forests
As they grind the mountains.
Come over me
Sense of time lying on its back.
Come over me
Mirrorless face, eyes without sight.

And now
Sleeping
Let sight come back into my eyes
Let ferric water wash them
Let eyeballs white as bone be clear
Let pupils grasp sight seeping through stone
Through cracks in the world above the world of the dead
Let hands grasp and pull at the roots
At daisy tails at the key to Solomon's seal
Let knees flex at the portion of rock that lies over them
Let chest expand against the weight, the cushion, the armor
Of bone and seed and tree
Let head and skull stir in the motion of waves in the sea of soil
Let worms burrow in the cracks of the ass and the cock
Licking clean
Preparing
Washing the body of soil, of nodules, of rot
Let body stir

Let hips bend and move
Let me rise like a swimmer dripping stones and humus
From buttock and flank
Let me walk knee-deep in salt grass and fern
Let me bend like a heron
Let me stir against tree roots like nut hatch and creeper
Let me spread across the meadows
Let me dry the moist stems of young roots
Let me climb the hollows in cold draughts of moonlight.

And now I see the ghosts of children
I see Frankie's son
Marshall, Paul
I see Kenneth and Dale
I see Harry, Robert
Winking through the shadows of sunlight
Naked little boys of four and five
Running together, holding hands.
This is harder than death,
Seeing this, remembering this that never happened
But will happen
Seeing it
Rushing with it over the moonlight mail of the dead
            Connecticut night.
Brown little bodies, rushing over sunlight
Playing
Twining thistles in the clean couch of empty noon,
Twining,
Turning brown,
Reasoning with death in their strong legs and arms
A circuitous death of reason.
Alive.